THE STORY OF
SIR WALTER RALEIGH

SIR WALTER RALEIGH

THE CHILDREN'S HEROES SERIES

THE STORY OF SIR WALTER RALEIGH

BY

MARGARET DUNCAN KELLY

WITH PICTURES
BY T. H. ROBINSON

YESTERDAY'S CLASSICS

CHAPEL HILL, NORTH CAROLINA

This edition, first published in 2007 by Yesterday's Classics, an imprint of Yesterday's Classics, LLC, is an unabridged republication of the work originally published by T. C. & E. C. Jack, Ltd. in 1906. For the complete listing of the books that are published by Yesterday's Classics, please visit www.yesterdaysclassics.com. Yesterday's Classics is the publishing arm of the Baldwin Online Children's Literature Project which presents the complete text of hundreds of classic books for children at www.mainlesson.com.

ISBN-10: 1-59915-216-9

ISBN-13: 978-1-59915-216-5

Yesterday's Classics, LLC
PO Box 3418
Chapel Hill, NC 27515

TO

ALEXANDER DUNCAN

DEAR XANG,

I know you love fairy tales and stories of strange adventure. The story of Sir Walter Raleigh's life is as wonderful as any fairy tale, and it is also true.

He lived in the days of Good Queen Bess, when the New World had just been discovered, and brave men were sailing forth to seek glory for their country.

Many Englishmen went to the New World. But Sir Walter Raleigh was the first who thought of making another home there for some of his countrymen.

He was one of the heroes who helped to make our little island of Britain a great empire with many lands beyond the sea.

This is why we shall never forget him.

Your loving cousin,
MADGE

CONTENTS

CHAPTER I

THE DEVON SAILORS AND THEIR STRANGE STORIES

MORE than three hundred years ago, a great queen, named Elizabeth, ruled over England, but the people loved her so much that they called her "Good Queen Bess."

At this time England did not own any lands beyond the seas. The Spaniards said that all the land beyond the Atlantic Ocean belonged to Spain, because the Spanish sailors had been the first to discover America. Every year they sent many ships to this New World to bring back to Spain the rich treasures they found there. This made the English sailors very jealous. They, too, wanted to sail across the sea, and to bring back gold and silver.

The bravest English sailors lived on the coast of Devonshire, in the south-west corner of England. These men of Devon hated the Spaniards more than any people in the whole world. If the Spaniards caught any English sailors in what they called the Spanish seas, they flung them, loaded with irons, into dark dungeons, and sometimes they tortured them. But this

1

cruel treatment did not stop the Devonshire seamen from sailing to the New World. It only made them more anxious to go and beat the Spaniards. They knew they were better seamen, and they thought they were better fighters, than the Spaniards. They used to say that one west-countryman could fight five Spaniards any day.

So they set sail for the Spanish seas, and boldly attacked the great treasure-ships. Sometimes they landed on the shores of the New World, and traded with the Indians who lived there. The Spaniards were very cruel to the poor Indians, so the Indians were glad to help an enemy of Spain. Sometimes the English "sea-dogs," as they were called, even attacked the Spanish ports, and seized the treasure as it was lying on the beach, ready to be shipped off to Spain.

The King of Spain was very angry, and asked Queen Elizabeth to punish these English sailors. He called them pirates, as indeed they were. But the English said that they were not pirates, because the treasure did not really belong to the Spaniards, since they had robbed it from the poor Indians by cruelty and torture. They said it was a good deed to punish the Spaniards for their wickedness. As for Good Queen Bess, she was proud of her brave sailors, and wore in her crown some of the jewels they brought back.

At this time, when so many Devon men were risking their lives for glory and for gold, there lived in a beautiful Devonshire manor-house a boy called Walter Raleigh. He was a tall, strong boy, with dark hair and bright brown eyes. He could box, and fence, and ride, and swim, and he knew how to manage a boat. He was clever, too, at school, and very fond of reading. But he loved best of all to listen to the wonderful stories of the sailors who had roamed in all parts of the world. All his spare time was spent on the shore, watching the ships and talking to the sailors.

Sometimes a sailor had a ghastly tale to tell. He had been captured by the Spaniards, and had been racked and tortured in Spanish dungeons. He could show his scars, and could tell, too, the wild adventures by which he had at last escaped.

Sometimes another sailor, with his fingers sparkling with jewels, and a Spanish dagger by his side, would tell how a little English ship had captured a great Spanish galleon, laden with gold and silver and jewels. He would show his velvet hat, in which a bird with glittering green and gold feathers was fastened with a golden clasp, and would talk of the strange country where such birds lived.

Often the sailors talked of a wondrous city, where even the roofs of the houses were made of gold. They had not seen this city, but next voyage they hoped they would. As they talked of it, their eyes sparkled, and one of them leaping up, shouted out—

> "Oh, who will join, jolly mariners all?
> And who will join, says he, O!
> To fill his pockets with the good red gold,
> By sailing on the sea, O!"

A SAILOR TALKED OF THE STRANGE
COUNTRY WHERE SUCH BIRDS LIVED.

Walter listened with beating heart. He longed to say that he would join. He longed to explore that marvellous New World. He longed to see that wondrous city. But most of all he longed to fight the cruel Spaniards, who tortured the brave English sailors and the poor Indian people. He knew that he was still too young to sail away to the Spanish seas. He had still much to learn.

But he resolved that when he was a man he too would fight Spain, and win glory for England.

As he turned from the beach to go home through the beautiful Devonshire lanes, he could hear the sailors singing—

"Westward ho! with a rum-below,
And hurra for the Spanish main, O!"

CHAPTER II

RALEIGH'S
FIRST ADVENTURES

WHEN Walter Raleigh was about fourteen, he had to say good-bye to his sailor friends. His father said that it was time for him to go to a great college in Oxford, where he would learn to be a clever man.

In those days there were no railways, so travellers had to ride or drive, which made the journey much longer. It took about three days to ride from Devonshire to Oxford, which is an inland place a great distance from the sea.

At first Walter felt very far away from his Devonshire home. He missed the sea, and he missed the boating and fishing. There is a river at Oxford, but that could not make up for the sea. He even envied the sailor lads who had gone to sea instead of to college. But he worked hard; and as he was very clever, everything he did was well done. He learnt Greek and Latin, which are very difficult. He learnt how to make fine speeches and how to write beautiful poetry. Everybody admired him, he was so handsome and brave, and soon he had many friends.

At this time, while the English people were so happy under Good Queen Bess, the people in France, which is just across the English Channel, were very miserable. The French people were fighting with each other, which is the most dreadful kind of war. Some of the Frenchmen came to England to ask the English to join their side.

When Raleigh heard of this, he threw down his books, and rode away with a hundred other Oxford men to fight in France. Raleigh was very young when he went to France—only seventeen. He stayed there for five years, fighting all the time up and down France. He learnt to be a strong soldier, always ready for the enemy, never taken by surprise. He was swift to strike, and swifter still to defend himself. He learnt how to command his men, and how to find out the enemy's weakest place.

When Raleigh came back from France he had his wish at last, and went to sea, but the book which he wrote telling of his adventures is lost.

All this time he had not forgotten his longing to fight the Spaniards. His chance came at last, though not in the way he had expected. There was no need to sail away to the New World, or even to Spain.

Many, many years before the reign of Queen Elizabeth, the English had crossed the Irish Sea and had conquered Ireland. But the Irish people were very brave. They were always fighting to drive the English out of their country, and now they had asked the Spaniards to help them.

News came to England that the Spaniards had landed in the south of Ireland, and were building a fort there. More soldiers were needed to put down the Irish rebels and drive out the Spaniards. This was Raleigh's chance. He was made a captain, and sailed to Ireland with a hundred soldiers, most of them brave Devonshire men.

On the sand-hills of a bay on the Irish coast the golden flag of Spain was flying above the fort, which held 800 of the enemy, both Spaniards and Irishmen.

Outside the sheltered bay the great waves of the Atlantic Ocean were dashing against the black rocks. But louder than the roaring sea sounded the cannons of the fort. They were thundering at the battery or little fort which the English had made among the sand-hills. Raleigh was in this battery, and his guns flashed back their answer to the Spanish fort.

"Down with that rag!" cried Raleigh.

The gunners fired once more, and the soldiers bent their long-bows at the hated Spanish flag which was floating proudly over the fort.

The flagstaff was struck! Down went the great flag of Spain. The hurrahs of the English soldiers were echoed by the sailors. For in the bay lay the English ships. The Spaniards were besieged both by sea and land. They knew that if they did not capture the English battery soon, all hope would be lost.

So on a dark stormy night 200 men stole silently from the fort. They were going to surprise the English.

They carried scaling-ladders with which to climb the walls of the battery. But in the darkness and the rain the way over the sand-hills was hard to find. Some of the Spaniards walked into the sea, and only just saved themselves from drowning! Some of them lost their way in the sand-hills, and had to wait until it was light enough to find their way back to the fort.

The men who did reach the English battery found the English ready for them. After a short fight the Spaniards had to fly for their lives. The next day a white flag was hoisted over the fort where the yellow one had been before. The white flag meant the fort had surrendered. The Spaniards were beaten, and could help the Irish no more.

But Raleigh's work in Ireland was not yet finished. The Irish were still fighting, and Raleigh had to stay in Ireland for two or three years longer.

There was in the south of Ireland a strong castle, which belonged to an Irish rebel lord. To this castle many of the Irish rebels used to fly in times of danger, knowing that the lord of the castle would give them refuge.

So Raleigh decided to try and capture the castle. He set out with only six men. They had a long distance to ride, along rough and lonely roads. On the way they had to cross a ford, which is a shallow place in a river. The men were very tired, for they had been on horseback for many hours. They were not riding together like soldiers, but were straggling behind Raleigh, some of them half asleep.

Suddenly, just as Raleigh was crossing the ford, there was a wild yell, and Irish rebels seemed to start up from every side. Raleigh was surrounded.

Then began a desperate fight, hand to hand. Raleigh, striking right and left, forced his way at last through the enemy. But looking back, he saw that one of his men was in great danger; his horse had thrown him into the river. He was struggling to get out; but in another minute the rebels would have cut him down. Quick as lightning Raleigh rode back to rescue his friend, who was a Devon man. Immediately the rebels turned on Raleigh. His horse was shot under him, and his enemies, with a shout of triumph, called to him to yield! But he stood with his pistol in one hand and a stout stick in the other, and held them all at bay, one man against twenty, until his friend was safe. Then, fighting his way through the wild Irish rebels, he himself escaped. He found that all his men were safe, and they marched quickly on to the castle; but all they found was a mass of smoking ruins. The Irish had burnt the castle rather than let the English capture it.

The story of his daring deed spread far and wide, even to the palace of the great Queen Elizabeth, who heard how one of her soldiers, far away on a desolate Irish bog, had fought for England single-handed against fearful odds.

Raleigh had many other desperate fights with the Irish. He had shown himself to be so gallant a soldier that he was often chosen to do the most difficult and dangerous deeds.

ONE MAN AGAINST TWENTY.

One evening he was told to take prisoner an Irish lord who had been pretending to be on the English side, but was really helping the rebels. This man, whose name was Lord Roche, lived in a castle with the strange name of Bally-in-Hash. It was one of the strongest castles in Ireland. Raleigh knew that it would be very hard to capture. But the very evening he received his orders he set out with only ninety men, promising that if he came back alive he would bring Lord Roche with him.

Lord Roche, who had spies all over the country, heard that Raleigh was on the way to Castle Bally-in-Hash, and sent 800 men to fight him on the road. But Raleigh went a different way, and so escaped.

In the early morning he came to the little town which was near the castle. Here he found 500 of the townspeople ready to fight him. But they were not real soldiers, and Raleigh, by pretending he had more men coming behind him, soon made them run away.

Then, leaving most of his men in the town, he hurried to the castle with only six soldiers. The other men were to follow.

"I wish to speak to Lord Roche," said Raleigh to the guard at the castle gate.

"You cannot enter the castle with more than two followers," said the guard.

"Very well," said Raleigh, going boldly through the great iron gate with only two men behind him.

He was taken to Lord Roche, who was sitting at breakfast with his wife in the castle hall. While Raleigh was talking to Lord Roche, the two soldiers, who had been left in the courtyard, managed to open the gate and let in all the other soldiers, who had now come up.

"My lord," said Raleigh, "you are my prisoner."

"Your prisoner!" cried Lord Roche. "You dare to say that to me in my own castle!"

Raleigh silently pointed through the open door to the courtyard, which was full of English soldiers armed at all points. Lord Roche saw that he really was a prisoner in his own castle.

When the night came Raleigh began the long march back with his prisoner. Again and again the rebels attacked him and tried to save Lord Roche. Again and again they were beaten off by Raleigh and his men. The night was wild and wet, and the way was steep and rough. But Raleigh kept his word. He brought his prisoner safely back.

For these brave deeds Raleigh was given broad lands in Ireland by the Queen.

But he was tired of Ireland. He wanted to go to London to see the great Queen and her lords and ladies. So he left his lands in Ireland, and sailed away to seek his fortune in London.

CHAPTER III

RALEIGH AND THE QUEEN

ON the banks of the great river Thames stood the palace of the Queen. The sun was sparkling on the river and on the pure white marble steps which led up from the water-side to the Queen's landing-place. At the steps lay the royal boat, gay with glistening white sails, and with the banner of England waving above it. The way from the palace-gate to the river-side was guarded by soldiers in scarlet coats with shining spears in their hands. These were the Queen's soldiers of the Guard. They were the tallest, strongest, and finest men in England. They were waiting for the Queen to come forth.

The palace gate was flung open. First came the gentlemen of the Queen's household. Then came the great Queen herself, followed by the lords and ladies of her Court. She looked a queen indeed as she passed, tall and stately, through the soldiers of the guard. She wore a dress of lovely satin embroidered with pearls. The bright jewels in her crown blazed in the sunlight. Round her neck was a ruff of costly lace; diamonds sparkled in her ears and on her breast.

Behind the soldiers crowded the people, who had come just to catch a glimpse of their Good Queen

Bess as she passed from the palace to her boat. They had given a great cheer when she first came forth, but now they were watching the brilliant procession in silence.

In the very front of the crowd stood a tall, handsome young man. His bright eyes were fixed eagerly on the Queen, as she came slowly towards him, smiling at the people as she passed.

The young man was Walter Raleigh, who was looking at last on the Queen whom he had served so well in Ireland.

As the Queen drew near the place where Raleigh stood she glanced at the ground and seemed to pause. Raleigh's quick eye saw that the ground at that place was muddy. Pushing past the guard, he flung from his shoulders his rich velvet cloak and spread it over the muddy spot. As he did so he bowed low before the Queen, his plumed hat in his hand, and the sun shining on his wavy dark hair. Looking up, he found the Queen was smiling graciously and thanking him for his courtesy. Then, stepping gently on the cloak, she passed on and went on board her boat.

Raleigh still stood where the Queen had left him. His face was glowing and his eyes were sparkling. Never would he forget this day when Elizabeth herself had first spoken to him.

Suddenly his thoughts were interrupted by a gentleman, who touched his arm where the muddy cloak was hanging.

STEPPING GENTLY ON THE CLOAK,
SHE PASSED ON.

"Sir," he said, "her Majesty has sent me to a gentleman who bears a muddy cloak. Will you please follow me?"

Raleigh, feeling as if he were in a dream, followed the royal messenger to the Queen's boat. The Queen was sitting with her ladies beneath a silken awning or shade to shield her from the sun.

"Sir," said the Queen, "we thank you for the offer of so fair a footcloth. What reward shall we give you?"

"I wish for no reward," answered Raleigh; "that your Majesty's foot should have touched my cloak is reward enough for me."

The Queen smiled. "What is your name?" she asked, "and where is your home?"

"Raleigh is my name, most gracious Queen, and my home is in Devonshire."

"Raleigh?" repeated the Queen; "we have heard that name before. Did you not risk your life to rescue your friend from the wild Irish rebels at a lonely ford beset with foes? Did you not fight and win, one man against twenty? We do not easily forget the daring deed of so gallant a subject."

"It was nothing," murmured Raleigh, with a blush; "no deed could be too dangerous in the service of your Majesty."

"You speak as bravely as you act," said Elizabeth, smiling again; "here is something to remind you always of this day." She gave him as she spoke a diamond ring; and Raleigh, kneeling before her, kissed her hand as he received it.

And that is the story that is told of how Raleigh first met Queen Elizabeth. From that day his fortune was made. The Queen never forgot her Squire of the Cloak, as she loved to call him. She even made him one of the gentlemen of her household.

The great lords and gentlemen, who lived near the Queen and were called her courtiers, were very jealous, because the Queen liked Raleigh so much.

One of these lords was called the Viceroy of Ireland, because he ruled Ireland for the Queen. He was very angry that Raleigh, who had only been a captain, should be given so much honour. So he said bitter things about Raleigh and tried to turn the Queen against him.

The Queen and the lords met together to judge between the Viceroy and his captain. First the Viceroy told his story. Then Raleigh answered him. He spoke so well that even the men who did not like him were forced to listen. All eyes were fixed on him. As for the Queen, she listened to every word he said as he stood there and told his story with flashing eyes and glowing words. She asked him many questions, and he could always give an answer. And when the lords saw how the Queen listened to Raleigh, it nettled them all.

So Raleigh was given more honour than ever. But sometimes he was afraid that all this good fortune would pass like a dream. He longed to become a great man and help the Queen to rule England; but he feared that in trying to gain more honour he might lose what he already had.

We are told that one day as he was thinking such thoughts as these, he took from his finger the diamond ring the Queen had given him. He was standing at the window of a summer-house in the Queen's garden looking over the river, and he wrote with the diamond these words on the window-pane—

"Fain would I climb, but that I fear to fall."

The Queen, who was walking in the garden with one of her ladies, saw Raleigh writing on the window. "We must read what my Squire of the Cloak has written," she said. "He wrote with the ring we gave to him; perchance what he wrote is for our eyes." Going to the summer-house which Raleigh had now left, she read the line. "He fears to fall," she said; "he fears to lose our favour? We will tell him that the man who wishes to be great must never fear."

So taking one of her diamonds she wrote on the window-pane just under Raleigh's line—

"If thy heart fail thee, then climb not at all!"

When Raleigh saw these words and heard that the Queen had written them herself, he felt both proud and happy. He knew she meant he was not to lose heart, but to go on striving to become a great man.

The Queen gave Raleigh many services to do for her. Every service was done so well that he was rewarded with lands and money. Every day he gained more honour and power.

One day he was called to the Queen's presence. She was seated on her throne in the great hall of her palace. The walls were covered with rich tapestry, which was silken cloth most beautifully embroidered in gold and silver and coloured threads by the hands of fair ladies. The hall was brilliantly lighted with torches of wax, for in those days they had no gas. The torch-light shone on the glittering armour, which hung round the hall.

But more brightly even than the polished armour sparkled the gay dresses and the jewels of the lords and ladies who were standing round the hall. It was a splendid sight.

As Raleigh entered, all eyes were turned on him. He was dressed in white satin, with a short close-fitting coat of rich brown velvet, embroidered with silver and pearls. His sword-belt also was of brown velvet. At his side he wore a jewelled dagger. In his hand he carried his velvet hat, with a long black feather fastened with a blood-red ruby pin. Even his shoes were sparkling with diamonds.

Kneeling before the Queen, Raleigh awaited her pleasure. She lifted a gleaming sword from her side.

"Walter Raleigh!" she said in a loud clear voice that all might hear, "In the name of God and Saint George, we dub thee Knight! Be Faithful, Brave, and Fortunate." As she spoke she struck Raleigh's shoulders gently with the blunt edge of the sword, and then exclaimed, "Arise, Sir Walter Raleigh!"

So Raleigh was made a knight, and every one thought how noble a knight he seemed.

It was a gay life at the Court of Queen Elizabeth. The Queen liked all her courtiers to wear fine clothes, and to be always gallant and merry.

She took great delight in music and poetry. So the young courtiers would sing sweet songs to please her, and make many a verse of poetry in praise of their maiden Queen. Some of these verses are so beautiful that they will never be forgotten. When Raleigh found that the Queen loved poetry, he was glad. He wrote several poems which gave the Queen much pleasure. Some of these poems are lost, but those which were kept show that Raleigh could write as well as he could fight.

In the evenings the Queen loved to have acting and dancing and "pleasing shows." Sometimes even in the daytime she would walk in her gardens dressed in fancy dress, followed by her pages dressed as woodland fairies. Often they would dance on the lawn, where the grass was kept as smooth as soft green velvet. Sometimes the Queen and her courtiers would meet together to watch the young knights show their courage and skill in arms at a tournament or mock-fight. The place where they fought was called the lists. The knights fought on horseback armed with blunted lances. They would gallop into the lists in shining armour with plumes of their chosen colour nodding on their helmets. Then when the signal was given they would charge each other at full tilt, and the knight who was unhorsed had to own himself vanquished.

At these tournaments Raleigh bore himself gallantly, and sometimes carried off the victor's prize.

The Queen made him Captain of the Guard, and so it was his duty often to be near her. He wore sometimes the uniform of the Guard, which was the colour of a golden orange, and was trimmed with fur. Sometimes he wore a suit of silver armour richly studded with diamonds, rubies, and pearls.

But all this splendour did not make Raleigh lazy. All day long he had to be at Court, but often in the evening he would read and study until the birds sang in the morning. He sat with his books in a little turret-room looking into and over the river Thames. This was his favourite room in the beautiful river-side house the Queen had given him.

In the autumn Raleigh used to ride away from the gay and brilliant Court back to his old home in Devonshire. The Queen had made him a judge over the Cornish and Devon miners. The judgment-seat was a very strange one. It was a great granite stone on a wild windy moor, far away from any house or cottage. Here the rough miners would gather round their judge and tell him their wrongs and their troubles. Raleigh listened patiently, and judged so wisely that the miners loved him always. Long afterwards, when he was in great trouble and many of his friends deserted him, he found these poor men still faithful.

So Raleigh had become one of the greatest men in England.

But sometimes in the midst of his busy Court life he would remember his old longing to win the strange new lands across the sea for England. He could not go himself, for the Queen would not spare the Captain of her Guard. But he was now so rich that he fitted out many ships and sent them to the New World. The adventures of Raleigh's sailors and their wonderful discoveries will be told in another chapter.

In the meanwhile news came to England which made every man, woman, and child wild with excitement. This news was so great, so terrible, that it even put a stop to the dancing and music and jollity of the Court. The Queen no longer wanted the Captain of the Guard to stay by her side. Every man in England was needed to fight England's greatest enemy. For the Spaniards were coming in all their strength to conquer these daring English people, who had so long defied them.

CHAPTER IV

THE SPANISH ARMADA

THE King of Spain had sworn a solemn oath that the English "sea-dogs" should trouble his sailors no more. No longer would he send messages to Queen Elizabeth to punish her pirate subjects. He was coming to punish them himself. The English were to be crushed once and for all. He would seize the crown from that proud maiden Queen, who had scorned his messages. He would give the fair lands of England to his greedy nobles. The gentlemen of England who dared to resist him should repent their deeds in dungeons, while the Spaniards feasted in their halls.

Stories were told in England of how the Spaniards had cut down whole forests to build great ships, larger and stronger than any ships the English had ever seen. These ships were called by the Spaniards the Armada, the Invincible Armada which could never be conquered, the Most Fortunate Armada which would always have good luck. Dark stories were told, too, of ship-loads of cruel scourges and iron fetters which the King of Spain was sending to punish his English foes.

No wonder the English people were wild with excitement. No wonder every man who could buckle on a sword was willing to fight. It was to defend their homes and wives and children they were called. No man could be a coward in a cause like that.

So the English kept a brave heart in spite of the stories of the Invincible Armada, which was to bring to their shores the strongest army in the world.

When Sir Walter Raleigh hurried to the west country to rouse and arm the Cornish and Devon miners, he found them willing and eager to fight the Spaniards. They flung down their pickaxes, and flocked to his standard shouting and singing—

> "Oh, where be these gay Spaniards,
> Which make so great a boast O?
> Oh, they shall eat the grey-goose feather,
> And we shall eat the roast O!"

In a very short time the whole kingdom was full of armed men, on horseback and on foot.

As for Queen Elizabeth, she was as brave as the bravest of her people. She rode through the ranks of the army on her beautiful white horse. She spoke to the soldiers with gallant words. "My loving people," she said, "I have come amongst you at this time to tell you that I would lay down for my God, for my king-dom, and for my people, my honour and my blood, even in the dust. I know I have the body but of a weak and feeble woman, but I have the heart of a king, and of a king of England too! I do not doubt that we shall have a famous victory over those enemies of my God, of my kingdom, and of my people!"

The soldiers answered with a ringing cheer. "God save Elizabeth!" they shouted; "long live our noble Queen!"

But the best way to beat the Spaniards was to beat them at sea before ever they could tread on English ground. This was work for the sailors, who were only too willing to fight the hated foe. It was Raleigh who advised the Queen to trust first to her ships. He knew the valiant seamen who had again and again routed the Spanish warships, and he hoped they would rout them once more.

One of the most daring of these sailors had indeed done harm already to the great Armada. This gallant man, whose name was Francis Drake, had sailed suddenly into a Spanish harbour, and had burnt and sunk all the ships he found there. This dashing deed delayed the coming of the Armada, and gave the English more time to prepare their ships.

On the coast of Devonshire, in a beautiful bay called Plymouth Sound, lay the English ships. They were not great iron-clad steamers as the English warships are now; in those days men had not discovered how to use steam to drive their ships over the sea. They trusted instead to the wind, and when their ships set sail they seemed like a flight of great sea-birds.

It was a warm summer day, and the captains of the fleet were on shore. Some of them were watching their white-sailed ships in the bay below, and talking together of the coming of the Spaniards. Some of them were playing a game of bowls on a smooth green lawn looking over the sea. There was Sir Francis

Drake, the terror of the Spaniards, throwing his bowl with as light a heart as if he had never heard of the Invincible Armada.

They are not afraid, these stalwart English seamen! They have fought the Spaniards in far-away Spanish seas; how much better will they fight in defence of their home and country! "Let the proud Spaniards come," they say, "they shall see what a welcome we can give them!"

> "Let them come, come never so proudly
>   O'er the green waves as giants ride;
> Silver clarions menacing loudly,
>   'All the Spains' on their banners wide.
> We shall sunder them, fire and plunder them,
>   English boats on an English sea."

Suddenly a small armed ship was seen running swiftly into the harbour under a press of sail. Her crew had great news to tell. The Armada was coming! They had seen it quite near the English coast. The ships, they said, were so many and so huge that they stretched over seven miles of sea.

At this exciting news the captains, who a minute before had been chatting lazily in the sunshine, began to hurry to and fro. They shouted for their men, and, hastening to the waterside, called for their ships' boats.

In the midst of all this excitement Drake had never moved from his place on the bowling-green; he did not even stop his game. "There is plenty of time," he said, as he aimed his bowl, "to win the game and beat the Spaniards too!"

And soon, gallant and gay as ever, these English seamen sailed out from Plymouth Bay to battle for their country and their Queen.

Meanwhile, swift horsemen rode inland to spread the news far and wide that the enemy had come at last. And when night came, a messenger swifter than any horseman was found to carry on the news.

On all the high hills throughout the length and breadth of England were lonely watchmen, waiting beside great piles of wood. They were watching for the signal to tell them the Spaniards were coming, and then they would light these great beacon fires to send on the news.

On a rock near Plymouth Bay shone the first signal flame. At once the fires blazed up on the cliffs along the Devon coast. Quickly the inland hills carried on the fiery signal—

> "And swift to east, and swift to west,
>   the ghastly war-flame spread."

The Spaniards, as they looked towards the England they had sworn to conquer, saw along the south coast—

> "Cape beyond cape, in endless range,
>   those twinkling points of fire."

And all night long the blazing fires sent on the warning that England was in danger—

"And on, and on, without a pause,
untired they bounded still;
All night from tower to tower they sprang;
they sprang from hill to hill."

Until, at last, all over England men knew that the enemy was near, and every village and town made ready for war, in case the fleet was beaten and the Spaniards landed on English soil.

But the English sea-dogs did not mean to be beaten. Though the Spanish ships were so great and strong, the English ships were much easier to manage; they could turn and move in every direction much more swiftly.

When the English came in sight of the Spanish ships sailing proudly along, they did not at once rush into battle; for the ships of the Armada were like floating castles, so great they were and so high. If the English ships had come to close quarters, and tried to board the Spaniards, they would have been broken to pieces. So, instead, they sailed just near enough to riddle the Spanish ships with deadly shot, and, turning swiftly, were away before the Spaniards could reply. Then they would dash in from another side.

Again and again the great Spanish galleons tried to get near enough to board the little English ships. Again and again the English sailed round them, and gave them no chance. So quickly could the English turn and sail that the Spaniards muttered that there were witches, not sailors, on board.

So the English chased the Invincible Armada away from England's shores. At last it struggled, battered and torn, but not beaten yet, into a French harbour.

Suddenly a crimson glow lit up the sea and land. The English had driven flaming fire-ships into the harbour. The Spaniards, mad with terror, struggled with each other to get out of the harbour and escape the fire.

Outside the harbour the English were waiting. Fierce and furious was the fight, but the English victory was sure. The Spaniards in their fear had lost all sense and order. Many of their greatest ships were sunk or captured.

At last all that was left of the great Armada fled northward, with the English sea-dogs behind them.

The English chased them until the English shot was all used up. Raleigh's ship was one of those which followed the longest. At last the English turned, and left the Spaniards to the stormy northern seas.

Wilder and louder grew the storm. On and on the Spaniards were driven by the wild wind, far out of sight of England, round the dangerous rocky coast of Scotland. Many of the ships were wrecked on the cruel rocks.

Some of the Spaniards managed to reach the shores of Ireland, and sought refuge there. But they were taken, and sent from village to village, coupled in halters, to be shipped into England. The Queen disdaining, as Drake tells us, to put them to death, and scorning to keep them, sent them back to Spain to tell the story of their Invincible Armada.

CHAPTER V

RALEIGH'S SHIPS

THIS is to tell how Raleigh tried to make another England in the great new land across the Atlantic Ocean.

Though the Spaniards said that the whole of this New World belonged to them, they only lived in a very small part of it. For America, as the New World is called, is nearly a hundred times bigger than Spain. It stretches from the frozen lands near the North Pole, where there is always snow and ice, to the sunny south, where there are strange beautiful flowers and bright-coloured birds.

The New World is really two great continents, which are joined only by a narrow strip of land. They are called North and South America.

The Spaniards had made their homes chiefly on the coast of South America, for it was in this part they had found the rich treasure of gold, and silver, and jewels. Here, too, they hoped some day to find the wonderful golden city of which the Indians had told them.

But Raleigh decided to make his new England in the unknown lands of North America. Here, he hoped, the brave, hard-working English settlers would become a great English nation, rich enough to trade with England, their mother country, and strong enough to fight her battles against the Spaniards in South America.

Raleigh had a step-brother named Sir Humphrey Gilbert, who was a very gallant captain and had already made several voyages to the New World. As the Queen would not let Raleigh himself go, Sir Humphrey Gilbert was made commander of the four ships which were to carry the English settlers to their new land.

They took with them food enough to last for a year, and all kinds of picks and spades and saws. The Queen sent Gilbert an anchor guided by a lady, as a token that she wished him good luck.

So the four little ships sailed west until at last they came in sight of land. It seemed to the sailors, who were looking for a rich and sunny country, a cold miserable place. It was an island, and round its shores thick fogs were always clinging. Off the coast lay a few fishing-boats. The Spaniards and Dutch had already found that there was good fishing near the shores of this land of fogs. The island had been called by its earliest discoverer Newfoundland.

Gilbert determined that, dreary though it seemed, he would take this island for England. He landed, and, cutting a sod of earth, he held it up and proclaimed: "The land from whence this sod is cut belongs from henceforth and for ever to England."

The captains of the fishing-boats stood silently by, while the English flag was set up on the shore. They had not dared to refuse Gilbert's invitation to go and see the ceremony.

But while Gilbert was on shore, his crews, who were angry and disappointed, tried to desert with his ships. One ship, indeed, Gilbert had to send home, but he persuaded the other three to sail with him further south, where the country would be warmer and richer.

Scarcely had they set sail when they were caught in a terrible storm. One ship was wrecked on the dangerous banks near the coast of Newfoundland; the other two ships still battled on against the winds. The sailors, terrified by the gales and fogs and huge sea-monsters, prayed to Gilbert to give up the voyage and sail for England.

The ship Gilbert was on was a tiny boat called the *Squirrel*. The storm became so violent that the sailors knew such a small crowded boat would surely go down. The men on both ships begged Gilbert to go on board the larger ship and save his life; but he would not. "I will not," he said, "forsake my little company with whom I have passed through so many perils."

The men on the larger ship saw him sitting calmly in the stern of the *Squirrel* with a book in his hand. As the two ships were driven for a minute nearer to each other, he called out, "Be of good heart, my friends! we are as near to heaven by sea as by land."

Soon afterwards the *Squirrel* sank in the raging sea. So died gallant Sir Humphrey Gilbert, and so ended Raleigh's first attempt to make another England over the seas. But the very next year Raleigh sent two of his captains to explore the coast of North America, and find a good place for English settlers. This time he did not send out any settlers; he waited to hear what his captains discovered.

These captains steered more to the south than Sir Humphrey Gilbert had done. They came at last to a green and beautiful land, a land full of tall stately trees, a land where delicious grapes grew right down to the water-side. Beneath the trees, shy, graceful deer were roaming, while the startled hares scurried swiftly to and fro.

The Indians who lived in this land were peaceful and friendly. The brother of the Indian king came to meet them with a band of Indians. They brought pearls, and corals, and deer-skins, to give the English in exchange for the curious things these white men had to offer. The king's brother was especially delighted with a tin dish. He hung it round his neck as a shield! Soon the captains set sail once more to take the glad news to Raleigh of the beautiful land they had found for him. Two of the Indians sailed with them to see the country from which these wonderful white men had come. They gave Raleigh a bracelet of pearls as big as peas.

Raleigh told the Queen about this new land, and asked that he might call it Virginia, in honour of his virgin or maiden Queen. She graciously consented.

SIR WALTER RALEIGH

Once more Raleigh collected great stores, and fitted seven ships to sail to Virginia. This time he prayed the Queen to let him go himself. But Elizabeth cared too much for his safety; she could not spare her Captain of the Guard to go a dangerous sea voyage.

So Raleigh was forced to stay at home, and send instead his cousin, Sir Richard Grenville.

Grenville took the settlers safely to their new home in Virginia. Then, when they had built their houses and landed their stores, he sailed back to England. He left behind him enough food to last a year, and promised faithfully to go back the next spring with fresh supplies.

The settlers worked hard. They had to cut down many of the great trees to clear their land. Then they ploughed their fields and sowed the corn. Some of them went exploring to search for pearls, and gold or silver mines.

The year went slowly by, and these lonely Englishmen longed for the spring. Spring would bring them news of dear old England, and all the friends they had left behind them. Spring would also bring the fresh supplies of food. This was even more important, for their food was running short, and it was not yet time to gather in the harvest.

Spring came, and the settlers watched eagerly for the sails of Grenville's ships. "He is sure to come; he promised, and he will not fail us," they told each other as the days went by and no ship came sailing to their lonely shore.

Spring passed and summer came; but still the settlers scanned the sea in vain with eager, hungry eyes and anxious hearts.

At last "A sail! a sail!" cried one of the watchers. But their joy soon changed to fear; for many sails came crowding over the horizon. Grenville, they knew, would only come with two or three ships; this was a large fleet.

"It is the Spaniards!" they whispered with white faces; "they have come to burn our homes and make us their slaves."

Great was their joy to find that it was not the Spaniards, but Sir Francis Drake, the terror of the Spaniards. He had been fighting the enemy in South America, and his ships were filled with Spanish treasure. He was now on the way home, and had re-membered to call at Raleigh's Virginia on the homeward voyage.

The home-sick settlers crowded round Drake's sailors, and wished that they too were going home. Drake loaded two ships with supplies, and said he would leave them behind him. So the settlers sat down to write their letters for Drake to carry home to England.

Suddenly a storm came on, and the ships with supplies were driven far out to sea. The settlers, in ter-ror at the thought of being left again in their loneliness and want, begged Drake to take them home. "Take us back!" they cried; "we shall starve before Grenville comes!" Drake could not refuse. So they left their wild but beautiful Virginia, left their homes to the wild beasts, and their corn to the birds.

A few days later Grenville's ships, laden with good things, reached Virginia, only to find empty houses and deserted fields.

Meanwhile Drake's fleet, with the settlers on board, sailed across the Atlantic home to Plymouth Bay. Drake's sailors brought back treasure. Raleigh's settlers came back poorer even than they set out; but yet they did bring home two things which afterwards turned out to be more valuable even than treasure. These were two plants—the tobacco and the potato plant.

Sir Walter Raleigh was bitterly disappointed that the settlers had deserted Virginia. But he listened to their stories, and examined carefully the two plants. They told him how they had seen the Indians smoke tobacco. "They suck it," said one of the settlers, "through pipes of clay, which does them great good. So we ourselves during the time we were there used to suck it after their manner, and found it of great virtue."

When Raleigh heard this, he thought he would try to smoke himself. A very funny story is told about Raleigh and his man-servant.

One day this servant came into the room where Raleigh was smoking. He had never seen any one smoke before, and when he saw smoke coming from his master's mouth, he thought he must be on fire! He rushed for a bucket of water, and flung it over Raleigh to put the fire out!

Raleigh liked smoking so much that he gave many of his friends pipes with bowls of silver; and soon all the young nobles of the Court learnt to smoke.

But as for the potato, no one would eat it at all. They thought it was poisonous, because the potato flower is something like the deadly nightshade. Raleigh thought this was a great pity, for the potato plant could be made to grow in England, and would be food for the people when there was not enough corn. Queen Elizabeth tried to make people eat potatoes. She had them served up at a grand dinner; but the courtiers only pretended to eat them.

So Raleigh took his potato plants to Ireland. He planted them there in the broad lands the Queen had given him. The poor Irish, who had little to eat, soon began to like potatoes. At last they spread throughout all Ireland, until every little cottage had its potato patch. But this, of course, took many, many years.

Raleigh's castle in Ireland had a beautiful garden. Here he planted sweet-scented, yellow wall-flowers which had come from Virginia far away. Here, too, he planted stately cedars, and cherry-trees, with their gleaming blossom. In a corner of the garden were four old yew-trees, whose branches had twined together, making a shady summer-house. Beneath these trees Raleigh loved to sit with an English friend who lived in an old Irish castle. His friend knew how to make most beautiful poems. Often the two friends sat beside the swift-flowing river, each trying who could make the sweetest song or tell the most charming story.

The name of this friend was Edmund Spenser. He was writing a most wonderful story-poem called "The Faerie Queen." This poem describes the strange adventures of many a gallant knight and gentle lady. It tells how a ramping lion rushed suddenly at a fair lady as she wandered alone in a wild wood; but when he saw how fair and good she was, even the lion was sorry for her and kissed her weary feet. Instead of devouring the poor lady, he became her faithful friend. Wherever she went, the lion went with her as a strong guard; and "when she slept, he kept both watch and ward."

As Raleigh read "The Faerie Queen," with its stories of dragons, horrible and stern, vanquished by true knights, he thought he had never read so marvellous a poem.

"You must come with me to England," he said to Spenser; "you must show your poem to our gracious Queen."

So they left Ireland and came to the Court of the Queen. She listened to "The Faerie Queen," and took such delight in it that often she called Spenser to her presence.

But Raleigh was tired of the Court. He longed for adventures, and when he learned that English ships were sailing west to fight the Spanish treasure ships, he implored the Queen once more to let him go. Once more she refused, and once more Sir Richard Grenville went instead in Raleigh's ship the *Revenge*.

The King of Spain heard that the English were going to attack his treasure, so he sent a strong fleet of fifty-three battle-ships to surprise them. The English had only six ships. When the Spaniards came on them, near the islands off the American coast, many of the sailors were on shore. To fight was useless, so the command was given that the English ships were to fly.

Sir Richard Grenville in his ship, the *Revenge*, waited to take on board the sailors who had gone ashore. "I would rather die," he said, "than dishonour myself, my country, and Her Majesty's ship by flying from Spaniards. I will force my way through both squadrons of them."

Swiftly the great Spanish galleons came sailing up and closed round the gallant little *Revenge*. The fight was long and desperate. All day long the *Revenge* fought on, firing low into the hulls of the galleons and smashing them through and through.

"And the sun went down, and the stars came out
  far over the summer sea,
But never a moment ceased the fight of the one and
  the fifty-three.
Ship after ship, the whole night long, their high-built
  galleons came,
Ship after ship, the whole night long, with her
  battle-thunder and flame;
Ship after ship, the whole night long, drew back
  with her dead and her shame."

But when morning dawned, the *Revenge* seemed like the skeleton of a ship. Forty valiant men lay dead upon the deck, and all the rest were wounded; all the pikes were broken, and all the powder spent. Sir Richard Grenville, sorely wounded but still undaunted, gave the command, "Sink the ship!" But his men insisted on carrying him from the sinking ship on board a Spanish galleon.

There he died, and his last words were as brave as his life had been: "Here die I, Richard Grenville, with a joyful and quiet mind, for that I have ended my life, as a true soldier ought to do, fighting for his country, queen, religion, and honour."

CHAPTER VI

WESTWARD HO!

AT this time there lived at the Court of Queen Elizabeth a beautiful orphan girl. Her father had been a wise and courtly knight. She herself was one of the Queen's maids of honour.

To Sir Walter Raleigh she seemed the most beautiful lady in the whole world. He thought, as he watched her waiting on the Queen, that he had never before seen so much grace and sweetness.

They often met, and every time Raleigh loved this fair maid of honour more and more. When he found she loved him too, he said they would be married at once. They did not dare to tell the Queen, for they knew she did not like her maids of honour to marry. So they were married secretly. But an enemy of Raleigh's told the Queen.

The Queen was very angry. They had no right, she said, to marry without leave from their sovereign. So bitter was her anger that she shut both Raleigh and his bride in prison in the Tower of London. After a few weeks, however, she was sorry, and gave them their freedom once more. Still she could not quite forgive Raleigh; she would not admit him to her presence or Court.

So Raleigh took his beautiful wife far away into the heart of the country, away from the glitter and rush of the gay Court life of which she was so weary. They went to the west country, where Raleigh had a splendid manor-house, surrounded by a great park with waving woods and grassy lawns. Here they spent two happy years, and in this lovely home their eldest son was born.

One day as they roamed through the woods, Raleigh talked to his wife of the resolve he had made when a boy. He told her of that wondrous golden city, for which the Spaniards were always searching in vain. He told her of his longing to sail westward and seek that city through the unknown pathless forests in the heart of South America. What a triumph it would be if he could only find it, and win such treasure for England! Why should it be left for Spaniards to find?

As he talked of the joy of wild adventures in strange lands, and of the glory that might be won in battles with the Spaniards, Lady Raleigh listened with a heavy heart. At first she begged him not to leave her. While he talked of glory, she thought only of the danger. But she was a brave woman, and when she saw how great his longing was, she told him at last to go.

So, after great preparation, he sailed away from Plymouth into the golden West. Once again he listened to the sailors singing their old song:

"Westward ho! with a rum-below,
And hurra for the Spanish main, O!"

But this time the voices were those of his own sailors, and Raleigh's heart bounded with joy as he thought that at last, after years of waiting, at last he was to explore the mysterious New World, and perhaps to conquer for England lands of untold wealth. He set out with five ships, and carried with him some small boats for rowing up rivers.

The land in South America to which Raleigh was going was called Guiana. Through this land flows a mighty river called the Orinoco. On the coast, at the mouth of the river, lies an island, which at that time belonged to Spain. To this island Raleigh came first. At night time some Indians came secretly on board his ships to ask the English to save them from the horrible cruelty of the Spaniards.

So Raleigh stormed the chief town of the island and captured the Spanish Governor. He set free the poor Indians, whom he found chained in dreadful dungeons.

Both Spaniards and Indians told Raleigh still stranger stories than he had heard in England.

"In a province," they said, "not passing a day's journey off, there are so many Indians as would shadow the sun, and so much gold as all yonder plain will not hold it. These Indians anoint their bodies all over with gold-dust to make the braver show, and then they dance, with eagles of gold hanging on their breasts. They are different from all other men, for the points of their shoulders are higher than the crowns of their heads."

Raleigh listened to these stories, but did not altogether believe them, for he noticed that no one had seen these wonders for themselves; they had all been told of them by some one else.

And now Raleigh made ready for his dangerous voyage up the Orinoco river. Leaving his ships at anchor near the Spanish island, he embarked a hundred of his bravest men in the five river-boats. They carried with them enough food to last a month.

The entrance to the Orinoco river was called the Serpent's Mouth, because it was so difficult and dangerous. Raleigh, describing it afterwards, said: "There are many streams, crossing each other so many times, and all so fair and large and so like one to another that no man can tell which to take; and if we went by the sun or compass, hoping thereby to go directly one way or other, yet that way also we were carried in a circle amongst multitudes of islands, and every island so bordered with high trees that no man could see any further than the breadth of the river."

Suddenly they saw in the distance a small canoe, with three Indians in it, crossing the river. Raleigh gave chase and soon overtook them. He persuaded one of the Indians to be his pilot. "But for this," he tells us, "I think we had never found the way either to Guiana or back to our ships."

Guided by the old Indian pilot they came to a "goodly river"; but so violent was the current, that they could row against it only by main strength, the gentlemen taking turns with the common sailors. When three days had gone the men began to despair. The weather was very hot, and the river was bordered with very high trees, which kept away the air, while every day the current seemed stronger against them. So long they laboured that many days were spent, their bread was nearly finished, they had no drink at all but the river water, and yet they seemed no nearer to the promised land.

The men, who were wearied and scorched, grew weaker and weaker. Raleigh had to persuade them to go on by telling them that one more day's work would bring them to the land of plenty. "If we return," he said, "we are sure to starve by the way, and the world will also laugh us to scorn."

On the banks of the river they found all sorts of fruit good to eat; but for this and the fish they caught they would have starved. There were many birds too of strange beautiful colours flitting about among the trees like great butterflies. Some were crimson, some orange, some a rich purple. The explorers were forced to shoot many of these gorgeous birds for food.

At last the old Indian pilot persuaded them to leave their biggest boat in the great river, and to row the smaller boats up a narrow stream. "It will bring you," he said, "to an Indian town, where you will find store of bread, hens, fish, and the country wine. This town is so near that you can go and return by night-fall."

So they rowed up the stream. For many hours they rowed, and still the pilot told them it was a little further. "But," says Raleigh, "when it grew towards night, and we asked where the place was, he told us but four reaches more. When we had rowed four and four we saw no sign; and our poor men were heartbroken and tired, for we had now come near forty miles."

Soon it was as dark as pitch. The river became so narrow that the trees hung over from side to side, their branches covering the water. The men were forced to cut a passage through the branches with their swords. They were very hungry, for they had eaten nothing since early morning, and had no food with them. They began to think that the pilot had led them that way to betray them. At last they decided to hang him as a traitor; but the poor old Indian kept telling them "that it was but a little further, but this one turning and that turning." Suddenly, soon after midnight, they saw a light, and rowing towards it they heard the dogs of the village barking. So the pilot's life was saved, and the weary sailors found food and rest for the night. When the day came Raleigh traded with the Indians for bread, and fish, and hens.

Then with this store of food they rowed back to their friends, who were waiting in the big boat or galley, as it was called.

They could now see the country which they had passed in the dark the night before. This is how Sir Walter Raleigh describes it: "On both sides of this river we passed the most beautiful country that ever mine eyes beheld; and whereas all that we had seen before was nothing but woods, prickles, bushes, and thorns, here we beheld plains of twenty miles in length, the grass short and green." Here and there groves of tall stately trees rose from the grass. "And still, as we rowed, the deer came down feeding by the water's side as if they had been used to a keeper's call."

In this river they saw many sorts of strange fish, "and of marvellous bigness." There were, too, many savage alligators. The alligator is a great creature something like a dragon. He is covered with an armour of bony scales. He has sharp, strong, cruel teeth. His mouth and throat are so large that he can easily swallow a man; when he swims he lashes the water from side to side with his great tail.

As Raleigh came near to the mouth of this river, where the galley was waiting in the great river, a young negro leaped out of the galley and swam to meet his master; but suddenly he was seized and devoured in their very sight by one of these dreadful alligators.

And now once more they toiled up the great river. They soon finished the food the Indians had given them. Once more they were nearly starving, when they saw in the distance some Indian canoes. They chased them, and the Indians in terror left their boats, which were laden with bread, and fled into the woods. But Raleigh captured them; and when they saw how kind and generous he was, one of them offered to be his pilot. So Raleigh gave his old pilot, who no longer knew the way, many presents and sent him back in one of the canoes.

Raleigh's men, no longer hungry, cried, "Let us go on, we care not how far!" So on and on they went.

At last, on the fifteenth day, to their great joy they discovered afar off the mountains of Guiana.

When the Indians found that Raleigh and his men were not cruel Spaniards, they came to the riverside, bringing them many presents.

Even the Indian king of that land came to welcome the good white lord. He was a very old and a very wise man. He came to Raleigh with all his chiefs behind him, each bearing a present in his hands. The old king had the strange name of Topiawari. He gave Raleigh a delicious pine-apple, which Raleigh liked so much that he called it the "princess of fruits that grow under the sun."

Among the presents which the Indians offered was a beast called the armadillo, which was barred over with small plates of bone, with a white horn growing at its back as big as a great hunting-horn; this horn was really the tail of the beast.

Raleigh took Topiawari into a little tent which he had set up on the river bank. There he told him that he was the servant of a Queen, who was the great chief of the north, and had more chiefs under her than there were trees in that land. "This Queen," said Raleigh, "is the enemy of the Spaniards because they are cruel and wicked. She has freed all the coast of the northern world from their slavery to Spain; now she has sent me to free you also, and to defend the country of Guiana from Spanish conquest."

THE KING GAVE RALEIGH
A DELICIOUS PINE-APPLE.

When Topiawari heard that the Great White Queen was an enemy of the Spaniards, he was very glad. All the Indians hated the Spaniards with fierce and terrible hatred. They told Raleigh the secret of how to make poisoned arrows, and how to cure the wound. These secrets the Spaniards had tried to discover for many years; but the Indians would not tell, even when they were tortured.

"I am very old," said Topiawari, "and Death calls daily for me. But if I am still alive when you return from the country of Guiana, I will come again to see you." So he said good-bye, and Raleigh and his men went on with their voyage in search of the golden city.

On they struggled against the current of that mighty river. At last they were forced to rest. They made a camp on the bank of the river and explored the country round.

In the distance Raleigh could hear the roar of many waters. He ran to the top of the first hill near the river, and from there he saw some wonderful waterfalls. Each waterfall was as high over the other as a church tower. The water fell with such fury that it looked like the smoke of some great town.

The strange thunder of waters drew them on little by little, until at last they went into the next valley, where they could better see the wonderful sight.

The country was very beautiful with hills, and valleys, and fair green grass. The ground was of hard sand easy to walk on. The deer were roaming on every side, and the birds, towards evening, were singing on every tree with a thousand different tunes.

Some of Raleigh's men brought to him pieces of white sparkling rock in which glittered some grains of gold; but the gold was deep in the rocks, and they had nothing to tear it out with but their daggers and fingers.

But now the heavy rains began, and the river began to rage and overflow very dangerously. The men, whose clothes were always wet, began to cry out that it was time to turn homewards.

So Raleigh had to give up his search for the golden city, but he decided that he would try again the next year.

The voyage back was very swift, for the current swept them down the river. They went nearly a hundred miles in one day.

Raleigh sent again for the old chief Topiawari. So many Indians came with him laden with baskets of food that it seemed like a great market in England. The hungry sailors crowded round, every one laying hand on what he liked; but Raleigh made them pay for everything they took, even if it was only a potato. So the Indians loved and trusted him more than ever.

Topiawari gave Raleigh his only son to take with him into England. An English boy called Hugh Goodwin, who longed for strange adventures, begged Raleigh to let him stay behind with the Indians. He said he wanted to learn the Indian language. One of the sailors said he would stay too to keep Hugh Goodwin company.

So Raleigh, giving them as much powder and shot and money as he could spare, bade them good-bye. He promised to come again next year if possible.

The journey back was swift and easy until they came to the mouth of the river, where it flowed into the sea.

Then there arose a mighty storm, and their tiny boats could hardly live in the raging sea; but at last they reached the Spanish island once more. There they found their ships at anchor, which was indeed a joyful sight.

"Now," said Raleigh, "that it hath pleased God to send us safe to our ships, it is time to leave Guiana to the sun, and steer away towards the north, home again to England."

CHAPTER VII

A FIGHT BY SEA AND LAND

EIGHT years had now passed by since the glorious victory over the Spanish Armada. Ever since that terrible defeat the King of Spain had been planning vengeance on the English. They had crushed him for the time, but some day his turn would come. With all the riches of the New World flowing into his treasury, he would make another Armada, stronger even than the first. Surely the gentlemen of Spain would then be able to conquer and destroy that race of sea-robbers. So he prepared once more a mighty fleet with which to invade England.

When Raleigh left Guiana he had promised the Indians that he would return the next year; but when he heard of the new Spanish Armada, he knew that he would be needed to fight England's battle at home, so he sent one of his faithful captains instead.

And now the Queen and her lords took counsel how best to save England and break the mighty power of Spain. They remembered Raleigh's advice, given eight years before, to sail forth and attack the enemy before ever they had left their own harbour. So they fitted out an English fleet, which was to attack the

Spanish ships as they lay in their own harbour of Cadiz, in the south of Spain.

News came to Spain that in the south and west of England great guns were being made, and many sailors pressed into service, and all England's warships fitted out.

But the proud, boastful Spaniards said, "These beggarly Englishmen are only seeking to defend their own shores."

At last all was ready. Once more the English fleet set sail from Plymouth Bay. As they left the harbour "there lighted a very fair dove" on the mast of one of the ships. "And there she sat very quietly for the space of three or four hours, being nothing dismayed all the while." The sailors were glad, for they said, "the dove will bring us good luck."

Among the brave men who manned the English fleet there were many who had fought in that great sea-fight which crushed the Invincible Armada.

But some of the bravest were missing. Sir Richard Grenville had died like a hero, fighting to the last for his country and his Queen.

Sir Francis Drake, the most daring of sea-captains, the terror of the Spaniards, was dead. The news of his death, far away in Spanish seas, had reached England just before the fleet started.

Yet there were still many gallant captains who meant to win a victory for England.

The chief commander was a dashing young nobleman called the Earl of Essex. He was brave as a lion, but not nearly so wise and skilful as Sir Walter Raleigh, who was one of the commanders under him. Raleigh did not like the Earl of Essex, who was very proud and vain, and often, indeed, rude to the captains who were under him.

As day dawned on a beautiful Sunday in June, the English fleet sailed into Cadiz harbour, with colours and streamers flying from every ship. Sir Walter Raleigh was left outside the harbour to attack any ship trying to escape.

Within the harbour lay a splendid Spanish fleet, ranged under the walls of Cadiz.

The English commanders decided to land the soldiers and try to capture the town before attacking the fleet in the bay. When Raleigh came into the harbour he found that the Earl of Essex was landing his men. The sea was wild and rough, and fifteen men had been drowned already.

Raleigh saw that all would be lost if they did not attack the Spanish ships before the town. So, in the presence of all the captains, he made Essex change his plans. The men were taken on board again, and the ships were made ready for battle.

Night fell, and the English commanders met to plan the attack on the Spanish fleet, which was to take place next morning. To Sir Walter Raleigh was given the post of honour. His ship, the *Warsprite*, was to lead the vanguard, which is the very front rank of ships.

All through the night, while the English were preparing for battle, the Spaniards in Cadiz were feasting and making merry. They had seen the English fleet sail into their bay, but they were sure that their own fleet would soon drive them out. The streets of Cadiz were brilliantly lit up with lamps, and tapers, and torches, and blazing tar-barrels. As the people sang, and danced, and laughed, they told each other, "We are quite safe, the great guns in our forts will shatter the English ships, even if our warships do not utterly destroy them."

With the first peep of day the English fleet, with all sails set and colours flying, sailed gallantly on to charge the enemy.

At the head of the English line came Sir Walter Raleigh in the *Warsprite*.

Beneath the walls of Cadiz lay the horrible Spanish galleys. The big ships or galleons had moved further up the harbour. The galleys were long snake-like rowing-boats. Each galley had about forty oars; each oar was rowed by five or six wretched slaves. A long gangway ran from end to end of the boat. Up and down this gang-way walked the slave-drivers with their cruel whips. At each end of the galley were soldiers with cannon and guns.

As the *Warsprite* passed the walls of Cadiz, the cannons of the fort and the guns of the galleys opened fire.

But Raleigh thought these galleys "but as wasps." "To show scorn to all which," he says, "I only answered first the fort and afterward the galleys, with my trumpet, disdaining to shoot one piece at any or all of those esteemed dreadful monsters."

RALEIGH GAVE THE WORD TO HIS MEN.

Leaving the galleys to the ships behind, Raleigh sailed swiftly on to where the great galleons lay. There was the *St. Philip*, the largest ship in the world, and many another huge galleon. Raleigh made at once for the *St. Philip* and the *St. Andrew*. These were the two ships which had boarded the *Revenge*, when Sir Richard Grenville fought his desperate battle against fearful odds, and died at last as a true soldier ought to do.

As Raleigh thought of that hero's noble death, he cried, "I will be revenged for the *Revenge*, or second her with mine own life."

So saying, he gave the word to his men, and a storm of musket-balls swept the great galleons. Thick and fast came the volleys of cannon. The fight was long and fierce. For three long hours the *Warsprite* fought both galleons at once. So quick was the firing that the three ships were wrapped all the time in a cloud of smoke.

And now the other English captains, eager to be in the thick of the fight, began to push forward, struggling with each other for the most dangerous post. One captain, indeed, secretly fastened a rope on to the side of the *Warsprite* to draw himself up abreast. But some of Raleigh's men saw the rope and told him. So they cut the rope off, and the captain fell back into his place behind the *Warsprite*. There, Raleigh says proudly, "I guarded him, all but his very prow, from the sight of the enemy."

At last the Spaniards in the *St. Philip* could fight no more. So, setting their ship on fire, they jumped into the sea to try to swim to shore. Another galleon was also blown up to save it from being captured by the English. The Spaniards flung themselves into the sea in heaps "as thick as if coals had been poured out of a sack." Many of them were drowned, and very few reached the shore alive.

Raleigh and his stalwart men captured two great galleons, one of them the *St. Andrew*. These were afterwards used as English warships.

It was a great sea victory for the English. After the battle the lives of all were spared, and they even tried to save some of the drowning Spaniards.

The Earl of Essex now landed and prepared to capture the city of Cadiz. An army of Spanish horsemen rode out to meet him, but after a short fight they fled back to the city across the sandy plain. The English followed, and found an old wall at the far end of the city over which they managed to climb. So the city was easily captured.

Raleigh had been badly wounded in the seafight. Yet he was so eager to help in the capture of the city that he made his men carry him ashore on their shoulders; but his wound was very painful, and he was soon glad to return to the *Warsprite*.

Sir Walter Raleigh was the first to bring the news of victory home to England. Great was the joy of all the people when they heard that the Spaniards had been beaten on their own shores.

The streets were crowded to cheer the victorious soldiers and sailors. A glad welcome was given to many poor Englishmen, who had been working as slaves in the Spanish galleys until the English victory had saved them from their life of misery.

When the people heard how Raleigh had led the fight, how he had answered the guns of fort and galleys with a blast from his silver trumpet, how he had seized the post of danger and captured two great galleons, they cheered him most of all as the hero of the fight.

CHAPTER VIII

RALEIGH AND HIS ENEMIES

RALEIGH'S little son, Walter, was now growing to be a big boy. But Queen Elizabeth had never forgiven his father, or allowed him to come to Court.

At last, as she thought how faithfully he had always served her and how gallantly he had fought for her, she began to be sorry. So she sent for her old friend, and made him once more Captain of the Guard. She talked to him very graciously, and in the evening they rode out on horseback together.

This made the other courtiers very jealous. The Earl of Essex especially was very bitter against Raleigh, and soon something happened which made him more bitter still.

The Queen sent Essex and Raleigh with a fleet to attack another town in Spain, or in the Spanish islands. Essex was chief commander.

Raleigh took with him the two galleons he had captured at Cadiz, which were now English warships.

They set sail for some beautiful islands, which lay in the Atlantic Ocean midway between the Old

World and the New.

Raleigh reached the islands first. He anchored in a pleasant bay before a fine town with a strong fort; this was the town they had planned to capture. They waited and waited for the Earl of Essex, and still he did not come. The men were thirsty, for their water had run short. They longed to land on that beautiful shore and attack the town.

After three days of waiting, Raleigh lowered the small boats, and they rowed towards the land. As they drew near the shore they were met by a deadly shower of shot from the fort. The men were afraid to go on, until Raleigh, rowing his own boat right on to the rocks, called them to follow their leader.

Climbing over the broken rocks and buckling on his armour as he ran, he dashed gallantly on, followed by his men, now brave enough for any deed.

They captured the fort and then the town, which they found deserted. The Spaniards had fled into the woods. The town was very pleasant, with gardens full of fruit and fountains of pure sparkling water.

Early next morning the Earl of Essex came sailing into the bay. He had been chasing a Spanish treasure-ship. Great was his surprise to find the town already taken, and great too was his anger. Raleigh had gained all the honour of the fight. For Essex there was nothing left to do. He dared not punish Raleigh, but he became his enemy for life, because Raleigh had taken from him all the glory of this "Island voyage."

When they returned to England, Essex tried to turn the Queen against Raleigh, but she would not listen to him.

Elizabeth was now growing very old. Her subjects began to wonder who would be ruler of England when she was dead. Her nearest relation was the King of Scotland, so most people thought that he would be the next King of England.

When Essex found that he could not make Queen Elizabeth hate Raleigh, he began to write many letters to King James of Scotland. James foolishly believed these letters, and soon came to dislike Raleigh though he had not even seen him.

Meanwhile, Essex tried to anger Raleigh in all the ways he could. On the Queen's birthday there was a tournament or mock-fight. Essex found out that Raleigh and his followers were going to wear orange-coloured plumes on their helmets; so to annoy Raleigh, Essex brought twice as many followers to the tournament, and they too wore orange plumes. He did this to make Raleigh's little band seem like part of his big one, and so he hoped to insult Raleigh in the presence of the Queen. But when the knights galloped into the lists and charged each other at full tilt, Essex tilted so badly that the people, instead of praising him, laughed at him.

The next day Essex came to the lists dressed in green. But he tilted even worse than the day before, and the people thought that the man in green was even sillier than the man in orange. So Raleigh had the best of it after all.

The Queen sent Essex to rule in Ireland, but he ruled badly, and came back to England without her leave. Elizabeth was very angry with him, and Essex thought that this was Raleigh's fault.

At last Essex became almost mad with rage and jealousy. He rode through the city of London at the head of two hundred gentlemen, crying, "For the Queen! For the Queen! To arms! Save the Queen from her evil councillors!" Then, as no one joined him, he called: "My life is in danger! Raleigh is plotting to kill me!" But the people only gazed at him in surprise, and no one took up arms for him.

He was easily captured, and put in the Tower; a few days later he was condemned to death as a rebel. And he was beheaded; for the Queen, even though she loved him very much, did not save him.

Raleigh's chief enemy at Court was gone, but many other men looked on him with jealousy, and tried to work him harm. But so long as the old Queen lived, her faithful Captain of the Guard was safe.

He was made Governor of Jersey, a rocky but beautiful island near the coast of France. So once more Lady Raleigh had to say good-bye to her husband. "Little Wat and myself," she says in a letter to a friend, "brought him aboard the ship."

This time the good-bye was not for long. The great Queen, who had done so much for Raleigh, was dying, and he felt his place was in England.

Brave in spirit as ever, Queen Elizabeth rode and hunted and held her Court almost to the last, trying to keep death away. But a day came when she lay upon her cushions too weary even to eat or speak, and soon the sad news travelled through England that Good Queen Bess was dead. Great was the sorrow of all her people.

Meanwhile, a greedy courtier, eager to gain the favour of the new King, rode northwards with all speed. At the royal palace of Scotland he knelt before King James, and offered him a "blue ring from a fair Lady." When King James saw the ring he was glad, for he knew that Elizabeth must be dead, and that he was now King of England.

As King James travelled to his new country, he was met on the way by many of Raleigh's enemies. They told him that Sir Walter Raleigh was a dangerous man. So King James came to England hating Raleigh more than ever.

Raleigh soon found this out, for the King took from him all the honours Elizabeth had given him; even his beautiful London house, with its gardens sloping down to the river Thames, was seized.

One hot summer day Sir Walter was walking up and down the terrace at Windsor Castle. He wore his great riding-boots and spurs, for he was to go hunting with the King. The sun shone on his gay hunting-cap with its long feather, and on the gold-embroidered cloak flung carelessly over one shoulder; but his face, as he gazed across the sunny fields, was thoughtful and sad. He was wondering, perhaps, how he could show the King that he was really a true and faithful subject, and that the stories of his enemies were false.

Suddenly a nobleman who was one of Raleigh's greatest enemies came from the Palace. He called Raleigh to the presence of the King's councillors. Raleigh soon found to his horror that he was accused of a terrible crime. A nobleman who had been unjustly treated by King James, had plotted to kill the King and make Lady Arabella, the King's cousin, Queen of England.

This man had tried to save himself by blaming Sir Walter Raleigh. He even said that the Spaniards had given Raleigh a great sum of money to persuade him to plot against King James.

The King's councillors, who were no friends of Raleigh, listened with dark faces to his angry denial of this shameful charge. A few days later a guard of soldiers carried Raleigh from his own house to the gloomy Tower of London.

In this prison he was kept for many weeks until the time came for his trial. The nobleman who had accused him was shut up in another part of the Tower. This man had once been Raleigh's friend, though he had now falsely accused him in his guilty fear of death.

To this poor wretch Raleigh wrote a letter begging him to tell the truth. On a dark foggy November night, Raleigh's faithful servant twisted the letter round an apple, and stole silently through the narrow passages of the Tower till he came to the nobleman's prison window. The window was open, so he threw the apple into the room. Soon he received a letter in return, which he brought to his master.

Raleigh read it with great joy, for it confessed that he was a true and innocent subject. A few days later fifty horsemen rode into the courtyard of the Tower. They had come to guard the prisoner on his way to the trial, which was to be in Winchester Castle, far away in the country.

All kinds of wicked stories had been spread among the people by Raleigh's enemies, and the very men who had cheered him as the hero of Cadiz rushed at his carriage yelling, "Down with the traitor! Down with the villain who sold his country to the Spaniards!" They would have torn him to pieces if the soldiers had not driven them off. But Raleigh sat, proud and calm as ever. At last, after travelling many days on roads thick with mud, they reached the old town of Winchester.

The great judgment hall in the ancient castle was crowded with people who had been waiting all night long to hear the trial. The Lord Chief Justice sat on the platform in a great satin chair. On either side were earls and barons.

There was a sudden hush as the prisoner entered. He faced his judges proudly, for he knew that he was innocent. But he had not much hope. The judges were his enemies, and he knew they would not judge him justly.

He had in his pocket the letter in which the traitor nobleman confessed that he had accused Raleigh falsely. But he soon found that this letter was useless. The miserable man had once more betrayed his friend. To escape from death he had sworn again that Raleigh was guilty.

"My lords," said Raleigh, "I claim to have my accuser brought here to speak face to face." But the lords refused; they were afraid that the traitor would not dare to tell his false story when face to face with Sir Walter Raleigh.

Then Raleigh stood up to answer the shameful charge which had been brought against him. He had spent his life in fighting for England against Spain, and now he was accused of being a Spanish spy. He reminded the judges how he had always hated the cruel Spaniards. Was it likely that he would join their side? "I was not so mad!" he cried; "I knew the state of Spain well. Thrice had I served against them myself at sea, wherein for my country's sake I had expended of my own property forty thousand marks."

As Raleigh pleaded for his life with burning words of truth, a thrill of sympathy passed through the crowd. One man said afterwards that "when he saw Sir Walter Raleigh first he was so led with the common hatred that he would have gone a hundred miles to see him hanged; but ere they parted he would have gone a thousand to save his life." But nothing could move the cruel judges or cowardly jury.

Sir Walter Raleigh was condemned to death as a traitor to his country.

CHAPTER IX

IN THE TOWER

IT was night, and the old castle of Winchester was dark and silent; but in one bare prison-room a dim light was burning. By the light of a flickering candle Sir Walter Raleigh was writing a farewell letter to his wife.

"My love I send you," he wrote, "that you may keep it when I am dead." Then he talked of what she must do for herself and her poor fatherless boy. He told her once more: "Your son is the child of a true man." Thus he tried to comfort "dear Bess," as he loved to call her.

This brave and beautiful lady, whom he had chosen and loved in his happiest times, was almost the only friend who had not left him in the time of trial. She was doing all she could to gain mercy for her husband from the King.

But all her prayers seemed in vain. Just when she had almost given up hope, news came that the King had decided to keep Raleigh in prison to the end of his days, but to spare his life. So Raleigh was carried back to the Tower of London, where he was to pass many long, weary years.

The great prison called the Tower is surrounded by strong outer walls. Within these walls stand, not one only, but many grim towers. One of them was called the Bloody Tower, because two poor little princes had once been murdered there. In this tower Raleigh had to live. From his window he could look over the river Thames and watch the ships and boats. The Governor of the Tower was very kind to Raleigh. He did everything he could to make the prison life easy for him; he even gave him his own garden, and allowed him to be there as much as he liked.

Damp and gloomy as the Tower was, Lady Raleigh begged to be allowed to live there with her husband. Her prayer was granted, so she and little Walter, who was now ten years old, came to the Tower, and made Raleigh's life there brighter and happier.

There was a little hen-house in the garden. Here Sir Walter spent many long hours making strange mixtures with drugs; he was trying to make a medicine which would cure all kinds of illness. He could no longer serve his country in battle, but he longed to work for it in some way. In the garden, too, he built a furnace, in which he could melt metals and find out what they were made of.

Sometimes as Raleigh walked in the Tower garden, crowds would gather in the street below to gaze at the great sailor who had explored the mysterious land of Guiana and fought so gallantly against the Spaniards. They no longer believed the wicked stories about him, so they were angry with the King for keeping him in prison.

Even the King's wife, Queen Anne, begged her husband to set Sir Walter Raleigh free. When James refused, she, too, was very angry. She went often to the Tower to see Raleigh, and brought with her young Prince Henry, the King's eldest son. Prince Henry was not at all like his mean and cowardly father. King James hated fighting and adventure; he could not bear even to look at a sword. But the young Prince loved all that was brave and noble. He admired above all men the great English sailors who had done such splendid deeds in the reign of Queen Elizabeth. Raleigh was almost the only one of these heroes left. Yet, instead of receiving the highest honour in the land, he had been thrust into prison. "No king but my father," cried the Prince with scorn, "would keep such a bird in such a cage!"

Prince Henry was especially interested in ships, and Raleigh told him the best way to build one. The Prince built a fine ship in this way, and admired Raleigh more than ever.

Often as Raleigh watched from his Tower window the stately ships sailing down the river, bound for the open sea, he thought of the days when he too had sailed the ocean. He remembered the dangers and hardships of a sailor's life, and he thought at last of a way in which he could make that life easier.

If sailors run short of fresh water when far away from any land, they either die of thirst or go mad through drinking the sea-water. But Raleigh, as he worked in his little hen-house with different kinds of water and drugs and melted metals, discovered a wonderful way in which salt sea-water might be made fresh.

A new trouble now came to Raleigh. Though all his riches had been taken from him, he still had his beautiful manor-house in the west country. There was, however, at the Court of King James a greedy Scotch-man who wanted Raleigh's house and lands. The King promised to give them to him. When Lady Raleigh heard this she was in despair, for she knew they would have no money left if they lost all their lands. So one day she went to the royal palace to plead with the King for mercy. She took with her young Walter and the lit-tle baby boy who had been born in the Tower. She knelt with the two children at the King's feet and prayed him not to take from those little ones their daily bread, and leave them without a home.

But James only thrust her away with harsh and cruel words. Afterwards Lady Raleigh was given a small sum of money to make up for the great sum of which she had been robbed. The King did this, be-cause he was afraid of what honest people might say of his dishonest deed.

Years passed by. Young Walter was sent away to the great University of Oxford. But still his father was kept in the Tower. The noble young Prince, who was always trying to help Sir Walter, became very ill. Queen Anne sent to the Tower for a bottle of Raleigh's medi-cine, which had once saved her own life. It was given to the Prince, but in vain. He died, and Raleigh knew that his best and most powerful friend had gone.

LADY RALEIGH WENT TO
PLEAD WITH THE KING FOR MERCY.

A new Governor came to the Tower, who built a great wall before the gate that the people might not gaze upon the prisoner. He made strict rules to make the prison life still harder to bear. For some time he would not let Lady Raleigh live in the Tower, and she had to take a house on the Tower hill to be near her husband. Raleigh himself was kept more closely in his prison rooms, and only allowed to go to the garden at certain times.

But though Raleigh felt that now that Prince Henry was dead he would never be set free, he did not give way to sadness and despair. He had always been fond of reading and study. Even in the days of his busy Court life he had found time to read. Now in his quiet prison he often read all day long. Some of the cleverest and most learned men in England loved to talk to this great prisoner whom the stupid King kept in the Tower. They brought Sir Walter all the books he wanted. They helped him, too, with the great book he had made up his mind to write. This book was to tell the history of the whole world from the time God made it to Sir Walter's own lifetime. It was brave of Raleigh to begin so great a history, for it is really a work which would take a man's whole lifetime to write.

After several years of hard work Raleigh finished the first part of the History of the World. Every one except the King thought it was a great and wonderful book.

The next chapter will tell why the second part of the History was never written.

CHAPTER X

RALEIGH'S LAST VOYAGE

FOR twelve years Sir Walter Raleigh was shut up in the Tower. During that time his glorious dream of a new England beyond the seas had come partly true. Englishmen had at last settled in Virginia, the fair land which Raleigh had named after Elizabeth, the Virgin Queen.

But Guiana was still an unknown country to the English, and Raleigh was always begging the King to gain some part of it for England. At first King James would not listen. He knew the Spaniards would be very angry, and he was very much afraid of the Spaniards. He wanted so much to be friends with the King of Spain, that his great wish was for his son to marry a Spanish princess.

But James and his courtiers were both greedy for gold, and when Raleigh told them of a rich gold mine in Guiana, they began to cast longing eyes across the sea. As Raleigh was the only man who knew the way to this gold mine, King James resolved at last to set him free and send him to Guiana for the gold.

When the King of Spain heard that Sir Walter Raleigh, his hated enemy, was free, he was filled with fear for the sake of his lands in the New World. He was so angry, indeed, that James nearly changed his mind after all. But his greed for gold was stronger than his fear of the Spaniards. He did not forbid Raleigh to go, but he promised the King of Spain that if any of his subjects were attacked in this search for gold Raleigh should be given up when he returned, to be hanged in Spain.

So at last Sir Walter Raleigh was free to leave the dark, dreary Tower and walk along the London streets in the sunshine of a bright winter day. He had been a strong man when the Tower gates had closed behind him twelve years before; now as he walked through London, looking curiously at the many changes in the well-known streets and buildings, he looked old and worn. He had suffered so much in his damp prison from the want of fresh air and exercise that he would never be strong again. His hair was snow-white, but his dark eyes still flashed with life and spirit.

Walter, Raleigh's eldest son, was now a brave young man, and his father made him captain of his own ship, the *Destiny*, which had just been built.

Every penny of the money which Lady Raleigh still had left was spent in fitting out the ships. Many other people gave money too to help in this exciting search for gold.

In the spring-time twelve ships set sail from Plymouth Bay. The weather was wild and stormy, and for many weeks the ships had to shelter in a bay on the Irish coast. A great sickness came amongst the crews and many of the best men died.

When at last they sighted the shores of Guiana, Sir Walter himself was too ill to leave his cabin for several days. In all the years that had passed by, the faithful Indians had never forgotten the great English chief who had treated them so kindly. Year by year they had looked for his coming, for he had promised to come again.

They flocked to the shore to welcome him, bringing many gifts. One of the chiefs, whom Raleigh called Harry, had spent two years in England, and had stayed in the Tower with his beloved master. He had gone back to Guiana, thinking he would never see Sir Walter again, and now his joy knew no bounds.

Raleigh was carried ashore, and his old Indian friends came in crowds to see him as he lay in his tent.

Suddenly a tall, fine-looking Indian pushed eagerly through the others, and knelt at Sir Walter's feet with an offering of Indian bread. His skin, though burnt brown with the sun, seemed fairer than that of the other Indians. He poured forth a stream of Indian talk mixed with broken words of English. What was Raleigh's joy to find that this was Hugh Goodwin, the English boy he had left with the Indians twenty-two years before! He was now a great man in his tribe, and had almost forgotten how to speak English.

This time Raleigh was too ill to make the dangerous river voyage himself. He had to stay at the mouth of the river with the large ships. He gave the command to a brave and faithful captain who had been with him in all the perils of his first voyage to Guiana, and who knew where the mine was. Young Walter Raleigh, his gallant son, was to share the command.

Raleigh gave them a month's provisions, and told them they were not to fight with any Spaniards except in self-defence.

For many days they toiled up the Orinoco River. As they drew near to the place where they expected to find the mine, they saw to their horror a new Spanish village. It was New Year's morning, and they decided to land and rest for that day, while they made up their minds what to do.

But the Spaniards, who had been warned of their coming, had laid an ambush. At dead of night, as the English lay sleeping on the river-bank, the Spaniards rushed down upon them from a hill and fiercely attacked them.

The Englishmen were so taken by surprise that they would all have been broken and cut to pieces had not their valiant captains roused them and led them on. As it was, they fought with such fury that the Spaniards were driven back. The Englishmen followed; but a new force of Spaniards came from the village to help their comrades.

For a moment it seemed as if the English would be beaten. But young Raleigh, calling to his men to follow, dashed on, and fearlessly charged the enemy. In the short but deadly hand-to-hand fight he killed the Spanish leader. He was wounded himself, but still fought on, bleeding as he was. At last he was struck down, wounded to death. With his last breath he cried to his men, "Go on!"

But even though their brave young leader had fallen, the English gained the victory and captured the village. The next day they carried his body to the little village church. All his men followed, and with the music of muffled drums they buried him there in that lonely foreign land.

The captain soon found that it was impossible to get to the mine. The men were very different from the brave Devon sailors whom Raleigh had commanded in the old days. And the Spaniards, who were hiding in the woods, sprang upon them at every turn.

At last the captain gave the word to return. So with heavy hearts they rowed back down the great river to tell Sir Walter the terrible news of their failure.

When Raleigh heard the miserable story he was almost mad with grief. His gallant son was dead! His men had come back without the gold. They had fought with the Spaniards, which meant certain death when he returned to England. No wonder, then, that he turned on the faithful captain with bitter words of anger. The poor man tried to tell him that he had done his best, but Raleigh would listen to no excuse.

The wretched captain was so heart-broken by the anger of his beloved leader that he could not bear to live; he went to his cabin and stabbed himself to the heart. So, at the saddest time of his life, Raleigh lost one of his most faithful followers in this miserable way.

The voyage back was very wretched. The seas were stormy; the sailors were wild and disobedient. Raleigh himself, sick and weary, was almost broken down with sorrow.

He wrote a sad letter to his wife, and sent it on by a swift ship to tell her the news of their son's death and his own ruin.

"Comfort your heart, dearest Bess," he wrote; "I shall sorrow for us both. I shall sorrow the less because I have not long to sorrow, because not long to live .... The Lord bless and comfort you that you may bear patiently the death of your valiant son."

CHAPTER XI

RALEIGH'S DEATH

IT was summer-time when the *Destiny* sailed at last into Plymouth Bay. Lady Raleigh had hurried to Plymouth, and was there to meet her husband. It must have been a very sad meeting for them both.

They decided to go to London and throw themselves on the King's mercy. But they had only travelled about twenty miles, when they met a messenger from the King who had orders to take Sir Walter prisoner; he had also been told to seize Raleigh's ship. So they had to go back to Plymouth, where they stayed some days while the King's messenger was looking after the *Destiny*.

Lady Raleigh begged her husband to escape while there was yet time. No mercy was to be expected from the unjust King. To escape would be easy while he was in Plymouth among Devon men and on the coast.

She pleaded so earnestly that Raleigh gave way at last. One of his old Devon captains engaged a French ship, which was lying in the harbour, to carry him to France.

At midnight Raleigh said good-bye to his wife, and stole from the house where they were lodging. On the beach he found the captain waiting for him with a little row-boat. They started at once to row to the French ship, which was lying some distance from the land to be out of gunshot.

Suddenly, when they were less than a quarter of a mile from the ship, Raleigh ordered the captain to turn the boat round and row back to the shore. Before he sailed to Guiana he had promised he would come back to England, and he must keep his promise. In vain the captain besought him to go on.

Sir Walter answered firmly that he could not fly; to fly would be to confess he was in the wrong. He had not kept his word by just landing at Plymouth. He must return and face his accusers.

So they rowed back to the beach. And Lady Raleigh, though faint with fear at the thought of her husband's danger, was prouder of him than ever because he could not be false to his word.

A few days later they set out for London with the King's messenger.

They passed through the green lanes of Devonshire, where Raleigh had played as a boy; and the men of Devon, who had always loved their great countryman, crowded to bless him as he passed.

The road led past the beautiful west-country manor-house where Raleigh had spent such happy years. It was to this lovely home he had first taken his young wife. Here, too, the brave son, who now lay in a

THEY STARTED TO ROW
TO THE FRENCH SHIP.

soldier's grave far away in Guiana, had spent his child-hood.

No wonder Lady Raleigh's eyes were dim with tears as she looked at the woodland glades and wide green fields where her boy had loved to play.

No wonder Raleigh, as he gazed for the last time on that beautiful park, exclaimed bitterly: "All this was mine, and it was taken from me unjustly."

Once more Sir Walter heard the great gates clang behind him as he entered his old prison in the Tower of London. This time his keepers even took from him the diamond ring Queen Elizabeth had given him, and which he always wore.

Soon afterwards poor Lady Raleigh was made a prisoner in her own house. So now, when her husband most needed her, she could no longer be with him.

Raleigh himself was never left alone, day or night. His guards were told to listen to every word he said, and repeat it to the King. They hoped to entrap him into saying something which might be used against him. They even opened and read his letters to his wife.

King James had resolved that Raleigh should die; but he did not want his English subjects to know that it was to please the King of Spain. Above all, he did not care to send Raleigh to Spain to be hanged. He knew that all England would be filled with horror and wrath. So for a few weeks the cowardly King delayed, and tried to find a new reason for killing Raleigh.

But the King of Spain, who was thirsting for the blood of his greatest enemy, began to send impatient messages to King James, saying that Raleigh might be beheaded in England, but it must be done at once.

James remembered how Raleigh at his first trial had turned the hatred of his enemies into sorrow and pity. This time James determined to judge him in secret, that he might not win the people's hearts again.

Very early on a chilly autumn morning Raleigh was roused from his bed. He was ill and very weak. They led him through the dark passages of the Tower to the carriage which was waiting to carry him to his secret trial. As they drove away he looked back for the last time on the grey battlements of the gloomy prison which had held him for so long. Weak and weary though he was, Raleigh spoke out as bravely as ever at this mock trial. But nothing could save him now. He was condemned to die.

When Raleigh heard that he was to die early on the next morning, he earnestly asked his judges one last favour. "My Lords," he said, "I desire thus much favour, that I may not be cut off suddenly; but may have some time granted me before my execution, to settle my affairs and my mind, more than they yet are. . . . I would beseech the favour of pen, ink, and paper. . . . And I now beseech your Lordships that when I come to die I may have leave to speak freely at my farewell."

But the judges could not put off the execution by a single minute. The cowardly King had hidden himself away in the country that he might not be troubled by appeals for mercy. Queen Anne had already tried to save her friend's life, but the King had roughly refused, and was resolved to be bothered no more. Raleigh must die, and at once.

After the trial, Sir Walter was led from the Hall at Westminster across the Palace yard to a small prison called the Gate-house. This building had once stood at the gate of a monastery, a place where holy men, called monks, had lived together. The monastery and the monks had been gone for many a year; but their little gate-house, where the poor and sick had come for help, still stood, and was now used as a prison.

In this place Sir Walter spent his last hours on earth. Many of his friends came to say good-bye, and one of them declared afterwards, "He was the most fearless of death that ever was known, and the most resolute and confident."

At dusk Lady Raleigh came to the old gate-house. She had hoped almost to the last that her husband's life might yet be saved. Her little twelve-year-old son, who had been born in the Tower, had written a pitiful letter to the King pleading for his father's life.

Already it was night-time, and she had only just heard that her husband was to die early the next morning.

She sat with him until they heard the great clock of Westminster Abbey strike the hour of midnight.

Raleigh told her that he could not bear to speak of their poor little son, so soon to be fatherless. He talked instead of what Lady Raleigh must do to defend his memory, in case he was not allowed to make a farewell speech before he died.

So he tried to make the terrible parting a little easier by showing his brave wife how she would still be able to help him. And because she loved him so much, Lady Raleigh kept back her bitter sorrow, though her heart was breaking. At midnight she tore herself away, and went out into the dark and lonely night.

Sir Walter was left to spend his last hours alone. The Lords had granted his request for pen, ink, and paper. He used them to write a last note declaring that he was innocent. Then in the stillness of the night he wrote in his Bible a short but most beautiful poem.

Early in the morning he was led out to die. He seemed bright and cheerful, and "made no more of his death," we are told, "than if it had been to take a journey."

The scaffold or platform on which the prisoner was to be executed had been put up in the Palace Yard. Early as it was a great throng of people had come to look for the last time on one of the noblest among Englishmen.

As they crowded near to see and bless him, Sir Walter noticed a poor old man without a cap. Taking his own cap from his head, he threw it to the old man, saying kindly, "Take this; you need it, my friend, more than I do."

He was allowed after all to make his farewell speech from the scaffold. He spoke for some time, and very earnestly. He thanked God he was to die in the light and in the sight of his countrymen, and not in darkness, nor in that Tower where he had suffered so much. Then once more he solemnly declared that he was innocent. And lastly he said, with a sad smile, "I have a long journey to take, and must bid the company farewell."

The executioner, kneeling down, begged Sir Walter to forgive him. "With all my heart!" answered Sir Walter, placing his hands on the man's shoulders.

Then he knelt down and laid his head on the block. The poor executioner could hardly bear to do his work. "What dost thou fear?" said Raleigh. "Strike, man, strike!"

The axe fell, and a groan burst from the crowd. The executioner lifted the head up and called "God save the King!" but there was no answering cheer from the people, who looked on in silent anger at the shameful deed. "We have not such another head to be cut off," muttered one man as he turned away.

All through England the story was told of how valiantly Sir Walter Raleigh had died. His very death became "a wonder and example." And the people looked with scorn on the craven King, who to please a Spanish prince had put to death his greatest subject.

Englishmen remembered then the glorious days of Good Queen Bess, when men like Raleigh had been free to fight England's battles and win for her new lands beyond the sea.

They remembered too how Raleigh himself had fought for the honour of his country in the weary waste of rebel Ireland, out on the broad ocean, in the New World, and even on the shores of Spain.

And some of them felt that the King of England would have to be taught that the lives of his subjects were too dear to England to be thrown away, as Sir Walter Raleigh's had been, cruelly and unjustly.